I Got The Swings

I Got The Swings

Eliza Stefanidi

THE **BLACK SPRING**
PRESS GROUP

First published in 2026
Eyewear Publishing Limited
The Black Spring Press Group (BSPG)
London, UK

Typeset with graphic design by Edwin Smet
Cover image by Getty images

ISBN 978-1-917788-62-5

BLACKSPRINGPRESSGROUP.COM

ELIZA STEFANIDI
was born in Liverpool in 1980 and currently lives in Athens
after studying ballet and Media and Cultural studies in
London. She is British-Greek. Diagnosed with bipolar
disorder at the age of 24, she has made issues of mental,
linguistic and social crisis her main themes. Her debut
collection, from Eyewear Publishing, was *Sleeping With Plato*.
Now a mother, she continues to write and explore many
creative interests.

TABLE OF CONTENTS

INTRODUCTION — 9

YOU KNOW — 13
THUNDERS FROM THE FLOOR — 14
WON — 15
MONDAY — 16
A DAY IN THE CLINIC — 17
TAKING ONE STEP TO FALL BEFORE YOUR EYES — 18
EVERYTHING COUNTS — 19
SOME YEARS — 20
THOUGHT CEILINGS — 21
YOU — 22
ALL — 23
SAFE — 24
EMPTY MOON — 25
AGAIN — 26
XI — 27
ALL AROUND — 28
SMILE — 29
TONIGHT — 30
APRIL TOWNS — 31
EVEN IF — 32
FOR YOU — 33
PENCILS — 34
SOME WORDS — 35
JUST WAITING — 36
CLOSER THAN NEAR — 37
UNTITLED — 38
NEW — 39
IN A DISTANCE — 40
FADED — 41
ONE MAKES TWO — 42
HEY — 43
AFTERLIFE — 44
JUST WAIT — 45
AN INSTANT STORY — 46

TALKING TO — 47

MONTHS — 48

UNTITLED — 49

O. YOU. — 50

ONE LAKE AND ONE RIVER — 51

NOTHING HURTS — 52

I KNEW TOO LITTLE — 53

FREE — 54

ABOUT — 55

NEVER MIND IT — 56

THIS WORLD — 57

A SIMPLE DREAM — 58

DOWN TO PIECES — 59

HANGOVER — 60

QUIET — 61

OUR STREET — 62

I CARE — 63

BROKEN — 64

NOVEMBER — 65

TIME — 66

STARING AT A YELLOW SUN — 67

THROUGH THE NIGHT — 68

COME ON LET'S STAY YOUNG TONIGHT — 69

BITTERSWEET — 70

HER HANDS — 71

THINKING NOTHING — 72

WINTER — 73

MONTHS MAKE YEARS — 74

THOSE CIGARETTES — 75

BY MY SIDE — 76

HEIGHTS — 77

YOUR FACE — 78

O CHILDREN — 79

9.3.2020 — 80

BACK TO BASICS — 82

NEARLY THEATRICAL I'LL WAIT — 83

FOR MY SON — 84

ACKNOWLEDGEMENTS — 86

INTRODUCTION

There is something I would like to share. It is an illness called bipolar disorder, in other words manic depression. Mine is type I. Here I am, home writing. It's June 2015. November the 12th, 2019. It's April the 9th, 2017, May the 21st. It was June 2004 when I first got diagnosed. Never knew what was about to follow. Never knew I would love an illness that never loved me.

I was born in a way that sometimes hurts. I'm almost normal, like you. In case you consider yourself normal that is. Or in case you too suffer from a mental illness, or facing mountains of pain for any reason you consider important. Through pain and tough times, through silence or darkness, through anything that threatens healthy brain cells and threatens life itself, I'm still here, you're still here.

I got the swings, I 'just' got the swings. These mood swings that have come after me for years and years. So here I am. On a bench, on a train, at a coffee table, at my kitchen writing my thoughts and views on my mental health. On my mental state and frame of mind. On my bipolar illness type I.

As I learned to accept, learned to love and embrace the 'voices', the psychosis, the racing thoughts, the hyperactivity, the lack of sleep, the manic or hypo-manic phases, the severe depression and what else follows, and what else lies in between. As I learned to accept me in terms of me.

I would listen to music locked up in my room, locked up in my emotional mind, locked up in my own tiny insignificant world and locked up in a phase that sometimes took months and months for me to recover to become normothymic again. That is normal, ordinary and 'well' with my typical dosage of mood stabilizers. It took one good, suitable verse to make things well. It takes Christmas songs, silence, loud stars in the sky, it takes one smile from my son to not just flip and drop and bruise any part of me.

It took Robbie Williams or Kurt Cobain singing on YouTube to become my life dreamers not savers. It took actors like Robin Williams and movies like *Silver Linings Playbook*, documentaries like Stephen Fry's *The Secret Life Of The Manic Depressive* to make me feel easy and comfortable with who I am. But most of all it took and still takes courage and strength and more strength to not just be swept by emotions and mood swings, by mania or hypomania and depression.

When motherhood is utterly the most significant aspect, more than any social stigma I find myself meeting, feeling trapped with neon signs of social stigma on my forehead and on my side, never helped me. No strings attached for happiness or sadness. For mood swings or unstable mental health conditions or problems can be fixed, need to be fixed, have to be.

Well, it's hard when you're in deep darkness to think about advice or medications suggested by doctors (if you're lucky to have them). To accept caring from your parents and friends (if you're lucky to have them) or strangers if you're lucky to meet some. It's difficult to stay in a room or a place, in an unfamiliar space and miss and love everyone apart from yourself. It's hard to suffer from a mental illness and face mountains of pain for any reason you consider important to have good and bad days and months and years in just 24 hours.

It is tough not to feel or feel numb, to feel a different version of self. And when you are a bit high to plunge right from up there in the sky and bruise your body and mind as much as you love hating yourself, as much as you love hurting or loving yourself. Where there is hope. Where there is. Dear reader, I got the swings.

YOU KNOW

You know since minds are even
shutting down yourself,
will only hurt your heart out twice

you know it goes in rough verses
when the absence of time
always needs time,

since minds are even
summing up yourself
will only dry your parts.

THUNDERS FROM THE FLOOR

Picking up the grey
to drive away,
slow.

With some lines of a movie.
Picking up the thunders
from the floor.

With some eyes fixed south.
When some days play loud.

WON

For all beds are damp and done.

For all the ends of ends have been won.

For all I care is for you; sitting there laughing

and humming words of a free-fallen moon.

MONDAY

Monday, February, Tuesday swaps the sun.
Heard you; under the stand of dizzy time & fun. Heard you;
spinning the corner of God's ache & care. O God made, God gave.
Reload rain, not pain. O please. Fun played.

A DAY IN THE CLINIC

Saw her dancing
on a white bed
with her white pale skin

barefoot to sing more pop songs
than her eighties

Saw her breathing
under an oxygen mask
with her voice covering the dusk
of my feelings.

And off my mind and off the light
she survived, we stayed alive
taking my hand to a memory

lane down the street
worth the ride.

TAKING ONE STEP TO FALL BEFORE YOUR EYES

We'll play the radio

stay up late, drink soft drinks, eat the walls,

hear the waterfalls on screens, breathe new sense,

try to rest, activate beginnings, feel new meanings,

get high with time, fall down like paper stars from

the sky. We'll play the radio and stay up late with no

cries, taking one step to fall, to leap before our eyes.

EVERYTHING COUNTS

Unfriend one month of the year,
block all ache that's nearer than near.

Unfollow shadows, their mirrors and their doubts.
Keep in mind he said, *everything counts*.

SOME YEARS

My eyes burn
it's you and the sun

Some years can melt down
some winters can break the ground

My eyes burn
it's you beneath a simple sun

THOUGHT CEILINGS

And; I'll try to.
Fall off thought ceilings
and not hail or howl.

And; I'll try not to.
Breathe new blood and
stop with some used thinking.

And; I'll try to act or function,
sit still, make coffee, (not) smoke
and stay thrilled.

And; I'll try.
And; I'll try not to.
I'll try for you.

YOU

You unfriend my blues. You block my darkness.
You; like *The Blue Danube* and *Carmen* in the
daylight. You. It's because of you.

ALL

All walking hearts on the line,
there must be a corner to hide with time;
to work just fine.

SAFE

Oxygen check, water most wanted

Wings to fly above ourselves

And greener lights, and greener grass

O dear keep us safe on the same side.

EMPTY MOON

Passed by to write my thoughts on your back
you said there's a difference when the story gets

dark. In a room, with an empty moon,
we stood like colours between the lines.

Dear somehow times can change
from time to time.

AGAIN

My hands get dry,
there's no room for a sky
I breathe your face
like a memory, try to talk,
forget to walk. Till the end,
before I mean what I
meant.

XI

Harmlessly gazing at pale rain windows like those
Mondays supposed to be.

'This city has constantly something fragile.'

'Those black and white films
must have had the essence.'

'It's them who think in mute that have freedom.'

When I thought of thinking and you went to bed in
my head with no frowns, some sun and few doubts.

ALL AROUND

It takes longer
to digest dark clouds
to return with a hello,

to say, 'never let go'
to raise the questions
and hear the answers.

It takes longer
to come down by your house
to create what's all about

to forget that
birds are flying all around.

SMILE

With some rain in her eyes
she turned back time
hurting his voice with her smile.

TONIGHT

There's more room to sing
than you think or you might

Oh God; you can fall for anything
like a child, tonight.

APRIL TOWNS

A thought of high
saves me from sipping memoirs.

As I linger for a delusion,
a reflection of a fixed smile.

And now April towns are almost out in the streets
with footsteps, with playback songs.

EVEN IF

Even if darkness becomes darker,

Even if we bound and break

Like thousands of tears make one sea,

We live like all roads begin and seem never-ending.

FOR YOU

You said you will walk beyond your mind
and fill the void with sense and time,

as you slept like a child with no pain,
and stood there with a warm cigarette

smoking out the game. There's no time
and no fear. What's left is what's near.

PENCILS

Under a blue rooftop on a summer night, you might

begin to hate what you like. And pull back your

thoughts and question the times of your life. And get

enough with rhymes and verses and pretend to

dance with all that's there and dry your face and

pencils. Under a blue rooftop on a summer night,

you might think everything is there without a might.

SOME WORDS

I fell on my knees to remember
some words to stitch a December
and you bare walked the moon

and then I left too soon.
As you drained your mind with time
and crossed your hands with this heart of mine.

JUST WAITING

Under the traffic lights

in between nights

I was waiting for angels

with letters in my pockets

and poems of the poets

to say how I feel

to miss how I kneel

to those years under the traffic lights

just waiting to be found,

waiting to start.

CLOSER THAN NEAR

The things that you knew well,
the storms you dried in a place called hell,
the smile you kept close to you dear,

the words you held closer than near,
the place where you walked free.
The story before the lines fell on me.

UNTITLED

It must take courage and more of something

for us to swim to the shore for nothing.

NEW

In the night
for some light

out of days
covered in blue

for some things
stay young

new.

IN A DISTANCE

Like a quiet voice

that burns the noise

written within

like all

somethings

about to begin

like a void in here

like you said you'll be near

quietly

faithfully

in a loud distance.

FADED

I'll breathe words and start to follow
when the roads get dark and narrow

and fade out with black and some pink
everybody's got a fixed heart to break.

ONE MAKES TWO

Sing slow to touch the moon

How close or far is too soon?

Flown away like rivers do

I'll be standing here where one makes two

With the wind taken south

In the night cut so loud.

HEY

For the skies burn bright.

They say things turn from left to right.

AFTERLIFE

Slow heaven's low,

Fall life is all.

JUST WAIT

Oh, wait to be heard through lenses and words
please wait; you know you can't carry all man's
weight flesh and bones.

Just wait; even if this world may be turning sick and
so wrong please stay; for rescue boats could
restart our living humming songs.

AN INSTANT STORY

Mocking birds on our doorstep. Windows may break

by hearing these couples's wedding vows opposite our

house. Church bells, trees, cars, buses, bicycles,

three white cats and an instant story of a time to fix

us before those windows break.

TALKING TO

Strangers in rooms full of ceilings,

all well-known matters must be heaven sent,

audience inhaling colored red feelings,

what could rhyme well this time?

MONTHS

Inhale.

Your mind is falling. Break the rain.

A night is calling.

UNTITLED

All rhymes can't rhyme right,
there's silence covering the light.

O. YOU.

Dragged the empty
and saved the honey dripping out of a violet moon.
Your coffee tastes like mine, like kids in the month of
June. Your ache hurts just fine. Your name. You. O. You.

Dragged the empty skies
on to the floor. It's nothing, it's something, it's much
more than a whole lot more. Scratched the empty that
follows the line. When nothing makes sense like this,
this time. It's nothing, it's something. It's you. O. You.
It's fine.

ONE LAKE AND ONE RIVER

It's a warfare war, it's a battle.
It hurts like one lake and one river near;
it hurts like an anesthetic dose of poetic poetry. It
must hurt like you are worried, buried three feet
under; it hurts like a well thought out joke. And he
said, don't even think about it, don't even. Don't
even close your eyes, there's a place to dream and get
around it.

NOTHING HURTS

All
dead ends
kept inside;
when 'nothing' hurts
like something
sometimes.

I KNEW TOO LITTLE

There's a place to remember; some stories made of
forever.
I knew, I knew too little. They say, angels die, demons
lie (somewhere) in the middle. There's a place to
remember. There's a God you've met and held in a
cradle. I knew,
I knew too little.
Think well he said, under your pillow.

FREE

Scratched the sun
came around
for a son

pulled my hair
cleared the sea
let me in he said,

I'm free.
Scratched the sun
bruised for fun.

Damp and taken.
Like seats reserved,
like smiles
in heaven.

Scratched the sun
turned the pages,
pulled my hands
tied up the laces.

Pulled my hair
cleared the sea
it's me he said.

Again.
So, free.

ABOUT

Headlights over headlines;
about 'young silence',
you won't understand
over truth or dare.

About zero gravity feelings,
above ceilings that lift my head.
Like hours, for hours kept inside;
like we all get fixed with some care,
sometimes.

NEVER MIND IT

This road sinks like it's shattered. Sings like it's
supposed to, and it; oh well, never mind it. Rights
and wrongs always argued, always mattered. And
your loud firm steps always echo in here. Like most
of us say never let go and let go, dear. And some
days are cut with violins; like days sewed with all
pretty smiles and runaways.

THIS WORLD

This world speaks in daffodils. Believes. It rests in peace, it rests in the midst of something. And under a pink full moon cares a little; strikes and goes south like a child caught up in a riddle. This world speaks. Believes. Drifts like some of us somewhere in the middle.

A SIMPLE DREAM

There's a fact, facts, computerized mathematics, maths, (more yoga mats), incorporated minds, bleached suns, young hearts, the f word governments, the lost governors, the found spirits, the solo beginnings. There are facts, like all that's there, all the compressed love that floats in the air, all the sickness that surrounds us. There is Meryl Streep today and Brad Pitt, there's your son or daughter you would like to meet. There's someone you lost in there and far out, there's a phrase like 'please take care' when there's always something about. There's more than meets the eye, when you could just laugh or even cry. And there is silence, as there has always been; and there's us to hang out, with some hope, a 'simple dream'.

DOWN TO PIECES

Waking up next to air
stepping above my head.

I can spill my coffee on the floor
on my hair. Down to pieces,

down low, like hundreds of young
kisses. When words spread words,

this world is floating; like heaven
cuts the night without warning.

Like now, I must be, must I be falling?
Yes, I am, I am falling.

HANGOVER

A piano and two electric guitars next to the door
a glass of water for the night on the floor.

I stayed for days and years in bed
pictures and post notes over my head.

One hangover that needs to be cured
one sometimes must sound like a fool.

With my figure erased by the light
in the night hanging out with another night.

QUIET

Numb like the wound you would like to try to cover.

Quiet like the rain you could dry and turn things

over. Don't you know nothing ever stops with fear?

I will dial your thoughts again, when you come

near. Numb, quiet like the wound you would like, to

try to cover. Swallowed like rain that falls down and

over. Like the rain that sometimes breaks. Like

music that sings and stays. I'll dial your thoughts

and come near. Nothing ever starts with fear,

nothing ever does, my dear.

OUR STREET

Evenings closer to madness,

I'll sip water and walk down our street for sadness.

And drive through my mind to scream and function.

Dreams through phones can talk less or more with

care and caution. Evenings closer to madness. I'll

sip words hold a cup with my two-bleached dry

hands. And glue a smile and get the feeling; no

skies can fall inside a ceiling.

I CARE

I can smoke for all of you,
with surprised sufficient air under my lungs.

Detached with the idea of some idea,
I care.

BROKEN

Glue your smile, the skies won't fall
Drink up, stay with cold statue words
Drink up, leave with suitcases that scratch the floor
And I'll drive for even and ever away.

NOVEMBER

And eyes can tell,
eyes can leak.

Homemade November,
we are thinking of forever.

Sharper than a half shadow in the sky
for we sit still, get high.

TIME

Those tears shook down
the line of a cold sterilized drain
and stood there;

as hays can shake
down any green
and lay upon eyes to break

or even breed
our blues and purples.
You know, it takes

someone to lose anything;
everything. It must take anything,
to love or sense everything.

STARING AT A YELLOW SUN

Crying is for the ladies,
dripping mascara bleached
with tears of joy,
not pain. 'For all of us not for some'
he sighed and
giggled.
'I apologize for the inconvenience,
thought you would laugh your heart out'…
As my pale skin synced into the sand
staring at a yellow sun.
And everything and everyone
paused their moments,
for the absence of time would only make them feel
younger.

THROUGH THE NIGHT

Drink up my face and I'll sip your tears right

through the night;

for there's an edge that cannot hurt us any further.

COME ON LET'S STAY YOUNG TONIGHT

Like faces in a concert crowd that sometimes

remember.

Like you and I play and pause a loud kind of

'forever'.

BITTERSWEET

Would you trust time this time;
and would you turn around to move on?

Will you believe in calendars and dates;
another bittersweet December ends.

HER HANDS

Hungry fourteen and sweet sixteen and cool twenties

and must have fifties. As she dived into cigarettes

and smoked the night, as others watched her hands

saving her life.

THINKING NOTHING

We ran with rain under our feet and kicked
memories like mud thinking of something.

When some arms tonight hold pain and others
the suns, we ran. With rain under our feet, thinking

nothing.

WINTER

This distance of time,
hiding behind a god's face.

As he stays up late to rest
and spring melts down a winter's taste.

MONTHS MAKE YEARS

I heard a feeling
counted your steps
walked through
took breaths, talked less
realised months make years
when some tears make tears.
I heard a feeling, roaming in the night
and then stood there beside the window
counting your steps
coming home, walking through.

THOSE CIGARETTES

I will quit soon where the roses grow.

And inhale the air you sipped with your tea
on my own.

Like youth gets flown.

I'll run or wait for hours on the phone.

I will soon quit where the roses grow.

And inhale the air you sipped with your tea
on my own.

BY MY SIDE

I heard you
through photographs
by my side

inside black and white films
the noir of the sixties
slipped through, behind my mind.

I heard your smile
inside your eyes

I heard you
through photographs
by my side.

HEIGHTS

Cold wind pressing my hood
let me in, somethings about to begin
beyond heights and cliffs, it's not summer or spring,

it's not even time to mend this life of mine.
Out in the cold, with air pressing my feelings
with green covering our ceilings,

beyond heights and cliffs, we will sing again.

YOUR FACE

Arms covering your face

we'll drive around, lay upon the ground,

hum for the hurt, listen to Kurt, pause the film,

close the doors in mute, silence the voices, pick up

the noises, throw our thoughts, keep our coats for

the cold winter. With arms covering your face;

there's a sky above with no filter.

O CHILDREN

Low; count low
the pain and the killing.

O children don't leave,
the riddles, their meaning.

Low; count slow
what's real is what's left.

O men don't fall,
thorns not treated, well kept.

Low; count low
the poets could write upon you.

Help, O God help;
little doves will sing for you.

Low; count slow
the scenes must play again.

O God don't go;
all men in heaven, in hell.

Low; count slow
O children, please laugh.

Low; count slow.

This world hurts
like it mustn't have.

9.3.2020

Today,
I'll switch
to a mother language
and stitch a 'Super worm'
moon in our kitchen.

And fill the sky
with trees, and fall
and break
and bleed and
wipe my knees.

For all, I care.
For all I do.
I'll cough my fears.
And sing for you.
Today; I'll march

with tears and
play those blues.
Today, I'll try,
like my super friends
say they do. And choke

on the news
and still pray for you.
Today; under a full moon.
Today, like no one's there.
I'll stitch my heart

with roses and stare.
Today, inside our home
with worn out ceilings,
I'll fall off my head
and swipe those feelings.

Today; with those church bells
damp, wet and done.
Today; where this world
hangs upside down
and still turns so wrong.

BACK TO BASICS

Sterilised
mathematics
could turn this world

into a case solution.
Feelings
could miss the point.

Hearts
multiplied by people
could fix this world.

Could make this
simple.
When all the above

won't make sense.
When all is complex
like insanity

that spins our heads.
Humans
above all; could make

this simple.
Ought to
make humanity

again;
through these times,
simple.

NEARLY THEATRICAL I'LL WAIT

and wait and weight your voice
that echoes your words
straight to my head.
Like this audience of yours.

Like this mind of mine
slipping from wheels
into heels as I kneel for a poem
and pretend it's mine.

Nearly theatrical I'll wait
and wait and weight the ways
to have faith for nothing is real
and real is everything.

FOR MY SON

My dearest, please remember that this is a beautiful world of melodies and hallelujah songs, of God's care and Mother Mary's shivered aches and love, of blossom Mays and wondrous eye-catching yellow rays and long-standing trees. Of anything you might like or anything you might believe. My dearest please trust what your warm English colour blue eyes can read and breathe. My sweet love, no matter what the others or I too might or have to say, no matter if all above sound boring or cliché; no matter what I can whisper or hum so wrong, please have faith my sweetheart, my loving son.

ACKNOWLEDGEMENTS

Thank to you Todd Swift, Edwin Smet, and the team at
Eyewear / Black Spring Press, for working with me to
bring this collection into the world.